PALESTRINA

Oxford Studies of Composers

Oxford Studies of Composers (7)

PALESTRINA

JEROME ROCHE

London

OXFORD UNIVERSITY PRESS

NEW YORK   MELBOURNE

Oxford University Press, Walton Street, Oxford OX2 6DP

OXFORD LONDON GLASGOW NEW YORK
TORONTO MELBOURNE WELLINGTON CAPE TOWN
IBADAN NAIROBI DAR ES SALAAM LUSAKA
KUALA LUMPUR SINGAPORE JAKARTA HONG KONG TOKYO
DELHI BOMBAY CALCUTTA MADRAS KARACHI

ISBN 0 19 314117 5

© Oxford University Press, 1971

First published 1971
Reprinted 1975 and 1978

Reprinted lithographically by Whitstable Litho Ltd, Whitstable, Kent
from copy printed by W & J Mackay Limited, Chatham

CONTENTS

I

INTRODUCTION

UNTIL recently, Palestrina was seen to stand alone in musical history as the great culmination of the age of polyphony that reached back to Dunstable and beyond. Baini's biography of him and Haberl's collected edition of his works, two of the earliest landmarks in modern musicology, heralded a veritable spate of nineteenth-century Palestrina scholarship. Even the appearance of the Lassus and Victoria editions early in this century failed to substitute a comparative historical approach for the isolated detachment of the Palestrina revival.

It has been only more recently, with the rediscovery and publication of the vast corpus of Renaissance polyphony by composers both great and modest, that we have had the means to assess Palestrina in his historical context. The object of this book is to project him against the background of his contemporaries and predecessors, and to show him as one among several great masters of the art of polyphony, working not in the high summer but in the autumn of the Renaissance.

Giovanni Pierluigi was born in 1524 or 1525 at Palestrina and, like so many other early composers, took his name from his birthplace. From an early age he was involved in church music, being a choirboy at Santa Maria Maggiore in nearby Rome in 1537. The age of the migration of Franco-Flemish polyphonic art to Italy was in full swing: the choirmasters at this church all bore names of this provenance, and Arcadelt may also have been one of the young Palestrina's mentors. His formative years must have been dominated by the excellent northern polyphony, for at this time Italy had not itself bred any church composers except possibly Costanzo Festa. His first appointment came in 1544, as organist and singer at the cathedral of his birthplace, where the man later to become Pope Julius III was bishop.

The remainder of his life, from 1551 onwards, was spent in Rome, though by no means all in the employ of the Popes. They gave him his livelihood as *maestro di cappella* of the Julian choir from 1551 to 1554 and again from 1571 till his death in 1594, and as a singer in the Pontifical choir for a short time around 1554. (The two choirs should not be confused: the latter was the Pope's private choir, which was also styled the Sistine choir; the former sang for public services in St. Peter's.) The intervening years took Palestrina to other appointments: from 1555 or so to 1560 as *maestro* at St. John Lateran in succession to Lassus; from 1561 to 1566 as *maestro* at Santa Maria Maggiore, where he had been a choirboy; and from 1566 to 1571 in the same position at the Roman Seminary. These three must have been among the highest Roman posts not controlled by the Papacy, but Palestrina maintained his connexion with the spiritual authorities by composing for the Pontifical choir, and receiving a pension from them. He also cultivated contacts with princes of both Church and state: in the 1560s he directed concerts at Tivoli for Cardinal Ippolito d'Este in the latter's fabulous villa, and had a Mass commissioned by Duke Guglielmo Gonzaga of Mantua. Palestrina, then, was a man of success. His two marriages also brought him financial prosperity, though he had to bear the blows of the death of his first wife and two of his three sons in the 1570s.

What of Rome itself, the centre to which he committed so much of his life? The story is one of gradual recovery from the wars of the early sixteenth century to the more settled environment of Sixtus V's pontificate in the 1590s, of the resistance to the reactionary powers of Spanish conservatism (even though Rome, as centre of the Church, was bound to remain traditional in outlook), and above all of the tacit acceptance of humanist principles typified in the new outward-looking approach of the Church. The Jesuits were the spearhead of this movement; unlike the austere Popes of the 1560s, they did not scorn secular art, but wished to bring education and enlightenment to ordinary people even if this meant simpler forms of expression. This view was reflected in the Church's encouragement, through the stipulations of the Council of Trent (1563), of clarity, simplicity, and an element of realism and even emotionalism in liturgical music. It is interesting to note that Palestrina was not in the Papacy's employ during the lean years of the 1560s, but was at the Roman Seminary, a modern institution created by the Council of Trent, where Jesuit ideals would no doubt have been in the wind.

The question that may concern us as we examine his music is how it reflected these ideals, how he was affected if at all by the Church's changing attitude to sacred music, and in what measure he could be said to be a man of his time. Given that Rome was a conservative ambience, it would obviously be unwise to expect to find Palestrina assimilating the most advanced techniques of contemporary Italian madrigalists; on the other hand it should prove illuminating to compare his work with that of his northern predecessors, from whom he learned so much, or that of contemporaries who were accepted in Rome, such as Victoria or Lassus or even Marenzio, a madrigalist but a Roman for all that. We should remember that Lassus and Byrd, the other two names commonly linked with Palestrina to represent the 'big three' of the late Renaissance, were far more versatile: Palestrina—like Tallis and Victoria—achieved fame through an output more or less restricted to sacred music.

In short, a comparative rather than eulogistic approach will be adopted, though one hopes that the result will not necessarily be the undervaluation that Reese remarked in more recent criticism of the master.[1] This comparative approach should apply no less in the treatment of various works within Palestrina's own output, a task hitherto rendered difficult by its centuries-old acceptance in toto as a homogeneous model for strict counterpoint.

[1] G. Reese, *Music in the Renaissance* (London, 1954), p. 459.

II

THE MASSES

I T is in Palestrina's Masses that we can best follow his stylistic development and witness the musical subtleties of his art. Historians have long been agreed that Palestrina's Masses form the central core of his output and contain his principal claim to excellence. It is the very emphasis on the Mass—textually the most abstract subject in this humanist age—in his output that distinguishes him from his contemporaries: his 105 works in the form compare with Lassus's 53, and with Victoria's and Morales's 20 or so each. Even before Palestrina, in Gombert's generation, the motet was beginning to attract composers more than the Mass, for they could choose the texts they set, illustrating the general mood and sometimes employing detailed musical imagery. While such tendencies matured in the music of Victoria, Lassus, and Byrd, they were foreign to Palestrina's aims. Hence his motets, even though there are some 250 of them, are less significant.

Most of the Masses appeared in thirteen volumes printed between 1554 and 1601, the last seven posthumously. It is difficult to be precise about chronology, particularly of the posthumously published works, some of which had been in manuscript for many years. It seems that, while the rate of publication increased later in the master's life, a fair number of the works were written well before their appearance in print, and our concern in this chapter will be to attempt an outline of stylistic development that may help us to date problematic works. To this end, a selection of eleven Masses will be discussed in some detail, the parody works (which account for half of Palestrina's Mass output) being left till last.

Of Palestrina's five canonic Masses, the most contrived and academic is the *Missa ad Fugam*[1] (Book II, 1567), in which both SA and TB are in canon throughout, showing Palestrina's obvious command of the more artificial devices beloved of his Franco-Flemish predecessors. The canon is always at the fourth, at a half-bar's distance, in all the four-part sections; even in the triple-time Hosanna, the canon persists at two beats' distance, resulting in superb cross-accents (Ex. 1). On the other hand the distance between the entry of the pairs varies: at the

[1] *Opere Complete*, ed. R. Casimiri and others (Rome 1939–), iv, p. 74.

Ex. 1

opening of each movement the upper pair state their canon first, followed by the lower a few bars later, in the Josquin tradition; but often
the pairs are closer, and where they share themes a close cohesion results.
This can be illustrated by a passage from the Gloria, whose sequences
again invoke the spirit of Josquin (Ex. 2).

Ex. 2 (bar 17)

Exx. 1 and 2 both end with cadences involving a double suspension
(asterisked) directly caused by the canonic writing. The implied parallel
fifths are rather bare, and it is interesting to note that Palestrina came
to eschew such writing—indeed double suspensions in general—in later
works. The Mass ends, as is normal in Palestrina, with an Agnus II for
one voice more than the predominant texture, in which an extra alto
leads the original one by three bars at the unison, and supplies an
English cadence (rare phenomenon) at the end (Ex. 3). That Palestrina
had learned much about symmetry and balance from Josquin can be
seen in the fact that both Gloria and Agnus II end with repeated material
(in the former bars 67–72 equal bars 62–66, and the theme has already
been used at bar 25 and bar 30; in the latter 'dona nobis pacem' at bar
17 is repeated at bar 31 with a varied ending) and that the opening of

Ex. 3

the Hosanna (Ex. 1) returns at the close, after a middle section that ends clearly in C.

The *Missa Brevis*[2] (Book III, 1570) is a transitional work. In some ways it is the most Josquin-like of Palestrina's Masses. The Kyrie, Gloria, and Credo all end with bold sequence phrases which are unlike anything else in his output; the outer parts often move together in tenths (e.g. Kyrie bars 26, 34; Credo, bar 138; Sanctus, bar 16; and Agnus II, bar 27); and some of the final cadences have the bold and exciting sound of Josquin's because of the parallel fourths in the inner parts (Ex. 4). The double changing-note in Ex. 4c is especially remark-

Ex. 4

able. But in other respects the *Missa Brevis* looks forward. Both sections of the Gloria, and Hosanna II, open chordally, and much of the melodic material of the Gloria is purely rhythmic in interest, with many repeated notes and voices paired together on the same words. There is the slowing down, as an expression of reverence, at the words 'Jesu Christe'

[2] *Opere Complete*, vi, p. 62.

(Gloria, bars 25, 62) and a descent through a ninth at 'descendit de caelis' (Credo, bar 47), by way of musical word-imagery. The overall impression is that Palestrina is here treating the words with the new respect which the Council of Trent encouraged. The five-part Agnus II is much richer than that in the *Missa ad Fugam*; where all five voices are employed we can often hear chords of five real parts. The final plagal cadence contrasts with those in Ex. 4 and represents, perhaps, the prototype of the Palestrina cadence.

As for a late work in four parts, there is no better example than the *Missa Aeterna Christi Munera*[3] (Book V, 1590). It belongs to the paraphrase Mass group, which comprises about one third of Palestrina's Masses, making it second in importance to the parody type. The paraphrase Mass is based directly on a plainsong, usually an antiphon or a hymn, each line of which provides the melodic outlines of imitation points used in various ways throughout the Mass. In his interesting study of Palestrina's Masses based on hymns,[4] Robert Marshall has provided evidence of date according to whether the versions of the plainsong used conform to Guidetti's *Directorium* of 1582 (which differ from earlier versions), and he confirms the lateness of the *Missa Aeterna Christi Munera*. He also shows how the fact that line 4 of the hymn is the same as line 1—giving an ABCA form—is exploited in the musical structure of the Mass. Thus the Sanctus has a cyclic form ABCABCA, where the two returns of A represent the Hosannas (though based on the same music, they are different settings) and the second BC represents the Benedictus trio.

The late date of this Mass is borne out by its conciseness and economy. Every movement is shorter than its counterpart in the *Missa Brevis*, which means that both Gloria and Credo can be through-composed without monotony. The Credo is scarcely longer than a lengthy motet, and the only verset for less than four voices is the Benedictus. A sense of clarity in articulation is present everywhere, whether in the ternary shape of the Kyrie, with the sections ending in F, C, and F respectively; in the plain four-bar phrase that Palestrina makes of line 3 of the hymn in Kyrie II; or in the Josquin-like repetitions between bars 6 and 12 of the Gloria or between bars 22 and 28 of the Credo. The slightest suggestion of word painting is present in the Crucifixus section of the Credo (bars 55–60) and later at 'vivos et mortuos' (bar 76), where the dead are represented by the low register. For variety, Palestrina introduces a short dance-like triple time for 'Et in Spiritum' (bar

[3] *Opere Complete*, xv, p. 1.
[4] *Journal of the American Musicological Society*, xvi (1963), p. 347.

83) and modulates out of the mode between bars 98 and 105. Throughout this passage homophony prevails, as so often in the longer movements of his late Masses. Unusually, the final five-part Agnus II is not canonic. Richness of scoring is less important here than variety of voice-grouping, another mark of the late Palestrina style. If the suave 6/3 chords at 'dona nobis pacem' come as a surprise, perhaps the highest admiration should be reserved for the sound of bars 39 and 40, where a syncopated tenor II runs against them, creating lush added-sixth chords (Ex. 5).

Ex. 5

The three four-part Masses so far discussed, though drawn from different periods of Palestrina's creative life, establish certain norms in the field of four-part Mass composition. What differences of approach can be found in four-part Masses by Lassus, Byrd, and Victoria? Firstly, the division of the Mass text and the incidence of versets for fewer than the total number of voices is not by any means uniform. Lassus may often have a *two*-part verset for 'Domine Deus Agnus Dei' in the Gloria and for 'Pleni sunt' in the Sanctus, an austere texture that harks back to Josquin; in the Credo he may have two reduced-texture sections, for different groups, starting at 'Crucifixus'. Byrd, in his four-part Mass,[5] adopts a more flexible scheme, writing much of the middle of the Gloria *à 3*, but changing the scoring from time to time. In his Sanctus, the 'Pleni sunt' is *à 3* following a full close, but dovetails nicely into the Hosanna. The Benedictus, however, is *à 4*. His Agnus is through-composed, setting both verses, whereas Lassus may set only one verse: if he does a second, the texture is swelled to five voices but canonic devices are not ubiquitous. As we might expect, Victoria conforms more to the Roman tradition of Palestrina.

Secondly, regarding linear writing and texture, Lassus is certainly more archaic in his Masses than Palestrina. The flowing style of his two-part versets allows of no word painting at the Crucifixus, for exam-

[5] *Collected Works*, i, p. 30, and *Tudor Church Music*, ix, p. 17.

ple. At other times the lines are more angular, with a propensity for octave leaps. In longer movements pair-alternation occurs, but block chords are more frequent in the Credo. All these devices mark Lassus as a direct adherent of the Franco-Flemish school of Josquin. Though it can be found at the opening of the Gloria and Agnus of his four-part Mass, Byrd uses pair-alternation only rarely, and chordal writing almost never. Individual lines are less angular than in Lassus, and octave leaps are usually avoided in treble parts. Victoria may often write more angular treble parts than either Lassus or Byrd, but the bass parts are most harmonically conceived in Lassus, moving largely in fourths and fifths in his Glorias owing to the prevalence of chordal writing.

Thirdly, in their approach to harmony and modality, Victoria and Byrd stand with Palestrina in their tendencies towards a major-minor key system; the more modal spirit of Lassus's Masses is yet another of his debts to his predecessors. Most of Byrd's cadences are either in the 'tonic' or make a half-close in the 'dominant', both with *tierces de Picardie*; they occasionally end in a 'relative major'. The very fact that one can speak in such terms is proof of Byrd's modernity. Victoria's use of false relations and extra-modal accidentals in the *Missa O Magnum Mysterium*,[6] for instance, is bolder than in Palestrina (Ex. 6a). The 7–6–5

Ex.6 A (Victoria: Sanctus)   B (Victoria)   (Palestrina)
Sa – – – ba – oth Ple – – ni sunt cae-   (lei) – – – – son.   (le) – – – i - son.

cadence that ends his Kyrie is warmer in spacing than Palestrina's in Kyrie I of the *Missa Aeterna Christi Munera* (Ex. 6b).

Warmth of writing is better sought in the five-part Masses of Palestrina than in the four-part ones, and it is worth noting that the former are almost as numerous as the latter in his output. If the *Missa Aeterna Christi Munera* furnished an excellent example of a late four-part Mass, another paraphrase work, the *Missa Beatus Laurentius*,[7] represents his mature achievements in five-part writing. A little-known Mass, it is based on a plainsong antiphon from the liturgy of St. Laurence, and was no doubt specifically intended to be sung in celebration of the feast

[6] *Opera Omnia*, ed. F. Pedrell, ii, p. 69.
[7] *Opere Complete*, xxiv, p. 194; unpublished till 1888.

of that martyr. The complete antiphon can be found in Agnus II (à 6) in canon between tenors II and III.[8] The three phrases of the chant are longer than in a hymn, and we normally find Palestrina using the first few notes of each for the principal imitation points, thus:

Phrase 1: Kyrie I, Gloria, Credo, Crucifixus, Benedictus, Agnus I and II
Phrase 2: Kyrie II, Qui tollis, visibilium omnium, Dominus Deus Sabaoth
Phrase 3: Cujus regni, Hosanna I and II

The only opening point deriving from another source is the Christe, which uses the later part of Phrase 1. Much of the Gloria and Credo is written in the decorated homophony that is so characteristic of late Palestrina. The words are heard with perfect clarity, and the only linear excitement occurs in the tenor parts at cadences like (Ex. 7). There are

Ex. 7 (Gloria, bar 51, 75)

many examples of warmth of colour, often involving a suspension whose resolution is already sounding in another part, and perhaps a soprano part moving contrary to the rest, as in the second of the two examples from the Kyrie[9] quoted in Ex. 8. These dissonances are not the kind of

Ex. 8 (bar 28, 42)

thing that books on the Palestrina technique tell us much about, except maybe as curiosities, yet they are such a feature of this work and of Palestrina's late writing in five parts or more that it is impossible to

[8] There is a misprint in bar 15, where tenor II should read D, B.
[9] See also Sanctus, bar 41, and Agnus II, bar 20.

dismiss them as contrary to stylistic purity. They are the harmonic events the ear perceives; they give the work its peculiar flavour. One might cite other 'irregularities': what are we to make of the semiquavers at bars 77 and 91 of the Credo? They are in fact written-out ornaments of a kind that might well have been applied indiscriminately by less tasteful singers in solo versets. What of the beautiful B flat in bar 5 of the Sanctus, quickly contradicted in the tenor? Or that flagrant breach of the regulations, an octave leap followed by a further upward movement, in the Benedictus (Ex. 9)? It may surprise us to learn that Palestrina was

Ex. 9   (bars 7-9)

qui ———————— ve – – – nit

able to break his own 'rules', but such is the prerogative of the mature composer.

Another important type of Mass in Palestrina's output is the tenor or cantus firmus Mass. Even in his youth, this type of composition was outmoded, which may explain why five such works remained unpublished during his lifetime, though they were probably early. The three published ones appeared by 1570. The *Missa L'homme armé*[10] (Book III, 1570) is the earlier, five-part setting based on the famous song: perhaps Palestrina, in adopting an archaic method of composition and a tenor of similar antiquity, intended to pay artistic homage to his Franco-Flemish forbears. Like the *Missa ad Fugam*, this is certainly the product of a period that had not yet witnessed the reforming spirit of the Council of Trent. The CF is generally laid out in long note-values, the unit of its triple time being one or one-and-a-half bars in the prevailing duple time; in Kyrie II, however, it moves faster than the other parts, its triplets creating unusual cross-rhythms. Only at the Benedictus does it migrate to the top part, and only at the Crucifixus is it absent. At the openings of all five movements the appearance of the CF is prefaced by imitative entries based upon it, but otherwise the contrapuntal fabric is made up of independent material, often triadic in shape so as to harmonize with the long pedal notes of the CF. Thus the Gloria and Credo have an almost totally polyphonic style utterly different from that in the later Masses. The only chordal passage in duple time comes at 'Et incarnatus' (Credo, bar 86), but even here the CF rings out beautifully as the other parts rest. Those who claim that the slowness of

[10] *Opere Complete*, vi, p. 97.

the CF renders its profane associations unrecognizable to the listener should examine the Hosanna, where all its merriment is present in the original, jaunty triple time, tenor II and bass tossing the melody from one to the other. The kill-joys of the Council of Trent had not yet pronounced, and there seemed to Palestrina to be no wrong in thus unashamedly quoting the song. At the opposite extreme is the serene end of the Gloria, its rising scales balancing the descending CF (Ex. 10).

Ex. 10

Mention must be made of several striking extra-modal passages (Gloria bars 59–65, Credo bars 54–70, and Sanctus bars 21–24 and 28–31) where Palestrina flattens the B natural of the Mixolydian mode by musica ficta or by writing in the accidental. This creates a 'minor' feeling that is archaic rather than modern (Dufay did it), but which certainly relieves any modal monotony. When handled like this in the Credo, the feeling of a sequential modulation is strengthened by the move from G to F in the CF, and by the harmonies (G–C–G moving to F–B flat–F) (Ex. 11).

Ex. 11 (bar 50)

The other cantus firmus Mass in Book III, *Missa Ut Re Mi Fa Sol La*,[11] belongs in some respects to Palestrina's middle period (it was in manuscript by 1563). The ascending and descending hexachord is generally confined to S II in a six-part texture made up, interestingly, of

[11] *Opere Complete*, vi, p. 216.

SSAATB; the lucid sonority of the four upper voices is exploited in the
Crucifixus and Pleni sunt versets, while yet another alto is added in
Agnus II to make a canon on the hexachord theme. Palestrina takes a
less detached attitude to the CF than in *Missa L'homme armé*; in fact
he makes liberal rhythmic divisions of each note to accommodate to the
text in the Gloria and Credo, so that these movements have a homophonic
texture that is surprising for its date, and contrasts with the thoroughly
contrapuntal feeling in earlier Glorias and Credos. The chordal tendencies of the Gloria culminate in a lively triple-time ending with second-
beat accents and a final hemiola cadence. The Benedictus introduces
the semiquaver ornaments which we noticed in the *Missa Beatus
Laurentius*, and also the rare phenomenon of an inverted double suspension at bar 35 (Ex. 12). The work has a strong sense of major tonality,

Ex. 12

being in the Ionian rather than the Mixolydian mode, even though the
CF consists of the hard hexachord starting on G. In the Kyrie, Sanctus,
and Agnus the approach to line is more conservative: lines are often
angular, opposing the stepwise movement of the CF, and texture is
thick, being made up of repetitions or superimpositions of short motives. This can be seen near the end of Kyrie I (notice all the descending-
fourth motives) or in Agnus I, where the figure

in bar 17 later becomes a kind of ostinato in the bass (bar 40 ff.), trans-
posed so as to harmonize with whichever note of the CF is sounding. But
perhaps the best example can be found in the Sanctus (Ex. 13). Having

Ex. 13 (bar 28)

announced the motive which then disappears into the fabric of the lower voices, S I sings an incredibly long melisma. Maybe it was because this pleased Palestrina so much that he repeated the whole passage from bar 40 onwards, thus giving some formal shape to the Sanctus. Another cantus firmus Mass, the *Missa Veni Creator Spiritus*,[12] resembles this one in its Gloria and Credo, in having the rhythms dictated by the text on the basis of melodic motion every one or one and a half bars, while in other movements the CF moves slowly, in the traditional manner. One is tempted to speculate on the possible doubling of such slow lines by instruments, so that the structure becomes clearer in these thick six-part textures.

The examination of the six Masses so far discussed—two early, two transitional, and two late—has shown that Palestrina's style is not something static. The fact that his music has been used for many years as the basis of an academic discipline has too easily led to its style being codified into a set of norms. Ever since the days of Fux the discipline has been obsessed with line and dissonance treatment at the expense of those aspects which can teach us more about Palestrina's stylistic development: the overall vertical harmony, handling of texture and sonority, and structure. At the same time it has caused his style to be viewed as the norm, compared with which those of Lassus, Byrd, and Victoria represented a deviation. If they are all regarded as equally valid, however, the dissonances in Exx. 8 and 12, for instance, will become a joy to the ear rather than a curiosity to the intellect. For there should be no mystique about Palestrina: he was just as capable of writing exciting clashes as any other polyphonist.

His later works, moreover, should not be viewed in isolation any more than the earlier ones, for they anticipate the coming Baroque in their undermining of polyphony. Respect for the text is achieved by the increasing use of homophony in the long movements; repeated notes, which become very common for certain parts of the Gloria text ('lauda-

---

[12] *Opere Complete*, xxv, p. 246.

mus te', 'gratias agimus', and 'Domine Deus' especially) are found at the openings of more elaborate movements, where they are laid out in the canzona rhythm:[13] 𝅗𝅥 𝅘𝅥 𝅘𝅥. Rhythm becomes more important than melody. The 3 + 3 + 2 syncopation beloved of Giovanni Gabrieli is subtly handled at the openings of the Kyrie and Gloria (the latter *chordal*) of the *Missa In te Domine speravi*,[14] while in the Gloria the acclamations 'laudamus te' etc. (bar 8 ff.) are given to the three upper and three lower voices antiphonally, bespeaking an interest in the Venetian manner of opposing sonorities. Movements more often open chordally, not imitatively: the locus classicus is the *Missa sine nomine*,[15] where all movements but the Agnus do so, and even the Crucifixus trio, which hardly contains any florid writing. It is hard to imagine this Mass —or, for that matter, any of the more homophonic late works in general —without an accompanying organ realizing the harmonically conceived bass line. The a cappella ideal of the High Renaissance was indeed fading.

We come now to Palestrina's parody Masses, and begin by examining two based on motets by earlier composers, in which his adaptations of the models can teach us much about his peculiar style. The four-part *Missa Quem dicunt homines* (Book VIII, 1599) is based on Richafort's motet first published in 1532, though the Sistine Chapel manuscript from which Palestrina probably worked dates from before 1520.[16] We are dealing, then, with a model composed two generations before Palestrina, in which imitative techniques are by no means fully worked out, dissonance treatment is comparatively unsophisticated, and the vitality and rhythmic exuberance of the individual lines are more important than the vertical harmony—all characteristics of Josquin's imitators of that time. The following table shows the precise sources of the musical material for Palestrina's Gloria, so that the reader may have more insight into the parody technique:

	Palestrina	Richafort	
b.1	Et in terra pax	Quem dicunt homines	b.1
b.10	laudamus te	respondens Petrus	b.11
b.27	propter magnam	quia caro	b.32
b.33	Domine Deus	non revelavit	b.38
b.42	Domine Fili	quia tu es Petrus	b.54

[13] See the Sanctus ('Pleni sunt') of *Missa Veni sponsa Christi* and the Hosanna of *Missa Vestiva i colli* (ibid., xxv).

[14] ibid., xxv, p. 131.

[15] ibid., xix, p. 168.

[16] Mass in *Opere Complete*, xxiv, p. 1; motet in *Das Chorwerk*, xciv.

b.49	Jesu Christe	sed Pater	b.43
b.54	Domine Deus	et ego dico	b.50
b.61	Filius Patris	Alleluia	b.76
b.74, 85	Qui tollis	Petre diligis	b.82
n.80, 90	miserere, suscipe	qui respondit	b.86
b.97	qui sedes	et animam	b.98
b.103	miserere	pasce oves	b.116(bass)
b.108	quoniam tu solus	ut non deficiant	b.125(alto)
b.114	tu solus Dominus	et ait Jesus	b.104(bass)
b.132	cum Sancto Spiritu	confirma fratres	b.140
b.137	in gloria	Alleluia	b.146(=76)

This shows how the two halves of the Gloria draw upon the respective halves of the motet, parodying its form as well as its content. An analysis of melodic leaps in the Mass shows that while the total proportion is similar in the Gloria and the motet (both are, incidentally, 151 bars long), Palestrina suppresses the bigger intervals and prefers thirds in the top part, though in the bass fourths and fifths are more abundant. Surprisingly, the Sanctus is *more* angular than the motet, especially in the top part. Another interesting fact is that full triads occur on less than one third of strong beats in the Richafort motet, but on half or more in the Gloria, Credo, and Agnus I of the Mass (all *à 4*); with only three voices in the Crucifixus Palestrina still manages the same proportion (32 per cent) as in the motet. The evidence is that even if he has to some extent preserved the contours of Richafort's lines, he has filled in the texture. He tends, furthermore, to render supple rhythms more four-square, gritty harmonies more spineless, and exciting melodies more placid, obscuring much of Richafort's clarity and boldness. For instance, the Josquin-like simplicity of the opening of Pars 2 of the motet seems watered down at 'Et iterum' in the Credo, the beginning of Agnus II, and especially the 'Qui tollis' of the Gloria (Ex. 14). Notice, too, how

Ex. 14

the final cadence is rewritten at the end of the Credo to give a complete final triad (Ex. 15). Only the mediant cadence of bar 11 of the motet is

preserved absolutely intact, occurring near the start of each movement. From a comparison made from the table above we can see how Palestrina may use Richafort's whole contrapuntal fabric, or he may extract a point—or one version of it, if Richafort has several adjacent ones—and weave his own counterpoint from it. An interesting application of this technique occurs in Hosanna I and II: Palestrina makes up the former (Sanctus, bar 45) of entries upon many variants of the 'pasce oves' idea (tenor, bar 115), only one of which is an exact replica, while in the latter he repeats the idea five times, setting quite new counter-melodies against it.

The five-part *Missa O sacrum convivium* has as its model Morales' motet of that name,[17] whose principal features are a smoothness of melody and a sense of contrast between slow and fast motion. It is written in a style that obviously has more in common with Palestrina's than does Richafort's. Palestrina's Mass is generally less melismatic; in adding a great deal of counter-material to that which is original, he shows a preference for a thick, warm texture and abandons Morales's economy of means. At the same time, he superimposes rather than alternates Morales' slow and fast motion, which sacrifices the clear articulation of the model. The most felicitous instance of this occurs in the Kyrie, where the slow minims, at first in the upper parts, pass to the lower (Ex. 16). Another quotation (Ex. 17) shows how the texture is

[17] Mass in *Opere Complete*, xxiv, p. 227; motet in Morales, *Opera Omnia*, ii, p. 115. The Mass was unpublished till 1888.

Ex. 17 (Kyrie, bar 28)

added voice

thickened by adding a new part below Morales' two original upper
voices. Several of Morales' richly-textured cadences are reproduced
more or less faithfully in the Mass, notably at bar 27 of the Gloria and
bar 24 of the Credo (= bar 30 of the motet), or bar 41 of the Gloria
(= bar 40), or the curious dissonance —an English cadence without the
flat seventh—at bar 32 of Agnus II, which has a precedent at bar 76 of
the motet, though the quavers are not exposed in the top part.

It is hard to date either of these two parody Masses, for the fact that
neither of the long movements in each has much homophony can be
attributed to the style of the models, and the overall length of the compositions would support the contention that they were intended for two
big feasts (St. Peter and Corpus Christi respectively). One is tempted to
assign the *Missa O sacrum convivium* to a later period because of its
definite tonal feeling and competent, assured handling of a rich five-part
texture.

In dealing with Masses in which Palestrina parodies his own works,
problems of stylistic transformation of the model do not of course loom
so large, and we can concentrate more on the compositional processes
involved in self-borrowing. The *Missa Dum complerentur* (Book VIII,
1599) parodies the Pentecost motet of that name published in 1569, but
in manuscript by 1562.[18] The motet is in a clear-cut responsorial form,
each of the two partes ending with the same thirty-three bars of music
and text (ABC/DC); in addition, each of sections A, B, and C ends with

---

[18] Mass in *Opere Complete*, xxiv, p. 117; motet in ibid., v, p. 149.

joyous Alleluias in a brilliant melismatic style which contrasts with the more syllabic verses that precede them. Once again, the Gloria follows the structure of the motet most closely, as the following table shows:

Mass		Motet		
b.1	Et in terra pax	Dum complerentur	Pars I	b.1
b.16	Gratias agimus	Erant omnes		b.12
b.21	propter magnam	Alleluia I		b.17
b.28	Domine Deus Rex	Alleluia I		
b.36	Domine Fili	Alleluia I		
b.43	Domine Deus Agnus	tamquam Spiritus		b.52
b.58	Qui tollis	Dum ergo essent	Pars II	b.1
b.82	ad dexteram	Alleluia II	I	b.41
b.88	miserere	et replevit	I	b.59
b.96	tu solus sanctus	sonus repente	II	b.18
b.104	tu solus altissimus	propter metum	II	b.12
b.110	Jesu Christe	venit super eos	II	b.31
b.114	cum Sancto Spiritu	tamquam spiritus	II	b.34
b.119	in gloria Dei Patris	Alleluia III	II	b.46

Although the texture of this movement is thick, Palestrina ensures that it does not become monotonous by using the periodic six-part tuttis that punctuate the motet as landmarks in the Gloria, and by carefully juxtaposing syllabic, chordal, and more florid material from different parts of the motet to preserve variety. On the whole the Mass is more ornamented than the motet, sometimes subtly so: in the short Hosanna the 'et replevit' tutti is rewritten to extend the canonic interplay in the alto parts, and the B flat cadence is forestalled by the extra few bars needed to end in F, even though the melisma of Alleluia III is preserved in T II (Ex. 18).

Another fascinating method of extending given material is Kyrie I, where the slow opening begins like the motet, but a new imitation comes

Ex. 18 (Motet, bar 59)

in A II at bar 3; at bar 8 it is heard in T II below intricate melismas and above more or less the same bass, and at bar 14 in T I with a new bass (Ex. 19). This new idea now dominates the music, and is itself set against

Ex. 19 (bar 14) (bar 20)

a third motive at bar 20 (A I), so that by the end of Kyrie I the music is no longer related to the motet, yet there is no lack of cogency in its argument. Its complexity contrasts with the simplicity found in the Crucifixus, which begins chordally and has a happy example of one voice leading the others, an English habit (Ex. 20). Texture is reduced

Ex. 20 (bar 82)

to four voices also in the Christe, Pleni sunt, and Benedictus, in the last of which different groups alternate, coalescing *à 6* at the end. Palestrina preserves the customary floridness of this section by selecting material from the Alleluias of the motet. This Mass is almost certainly not a late work, for it dwells mainly on the linear brilliance of its model, ignoring its more homophonic aspects.

Palestrina's four Masses for double choir, published at Venice in 1601, were all modelled upon his own motets. The festive *Missa Hodie Christus natus est* in particular was derived from the Christmas motet published in 1575.[19] The parody here is of a less tangible sort, for although the basic textural procedures—such as stating material on one choir, repeating it on the other and combining the two in a tutti—and the inherent contrast of colour between the two choirs (SSAB versus ATTB), are preserved, there is not much in the way of detailed re-composition. To proceed as the motet does, with scarcely any imitative writing, would hardly be appropriate for a complete Mass setting, so Palestrina often selects an occasional motive from one voice in a less syllabic part of the motet and weaves a new imitative texture from it. Thus the sturdy bass line at bar 42 of the motet is so treated in Kyrie II and at 'Qui tollis' in the Gloria; the 'gloria' idea in S I and T I in bar 53 turns up at 'qui sedes' (bar 81 of Gloria), the melismas of 'laetantur' (bar 34) are used in the Credo at bar 113 and in the Benedictus at bar 23, and the Hosanna point is derived from the bass in bars 41–2. As for the chords at the opening of the Christe, they are extracted from bars 21–2, like the melisma that follows them (Ex. 21). Otherwise the short,

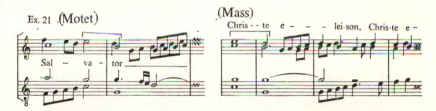

Ex. 21 .(Motet)   .(Mass)

clipped phrases of the motet have to be extended considerably to cover the more verbose Mass text, and there is little close resemblance between Mass and model in the longer movements. To compensate for this, the spirit of the motet is certainly invoked by the use of joyous triple time to end each movement (except the Agnus) in the manner of the model. The idea of a periodic massed tutti, ending on G or C cadences, helps to shape the structure in the Gloria and Credo, and is extended in the

[19] Mass in *Opere Complete*, xxx, p. 59; motet in ibid., viii, p. 202.

Sanctus so that the tuttis serve to sum up the previous alternating music. Here the joins are neatly dovetailed, and the chordal clarity of the motet is put aside in favour of a complex web of sound. It is, paradoxically, in a four-part verset that some of the simplest homophonic writing can be found ('et iterum' in the Credo). Altogether, this Mass is less a parody than a work in its own right, sharing the festive spirit of the model through harmonic, modal, and textural colouring, yet conceived on a more expansive scale. Written in a thoroughly modern Venetian manner, it is appropriate that it should have been published in Venice: such music was most fashionable among choirs where double-choir singing was the order of the day.

There is no need to examine closely the parody technique in the superb *Missa Assumpta est Maria*,[20] for its own qualities tell us enough about the maturity and genius to be found in its composer's last works. Here vitality of line is combined with an attention to vertical sonority and grouping that prefigures the Baroque, while at the same time Palestrina seems to have regained the classical sense of clarity and articulation which were the hallmark of Josquin and his school, and which he had sacrificed in some earlier works. Far from being elaborate contrapuntal movements, the Kyrie and Agnus have a mainly textural interest, contrasting different densities and groupings of the six voices. All of their component sections open chordally except Kyrie I, and the Kyrie ends with a particularly fine example of register contrast between upper and lower voices leading to a tutti, in the best *cori spezzati* fashion (Ex. 22). The end of the Credo provides a similar example. Both the

Ex. 22

Gloria and Credo are harmonically conceived, elaboration being confined to short melismas or syncopated inner parts; an almost baroque boldness inspires the sudden D major of 'Gratias' (bar 16) or the B flat major of 'miserere' (bar 64), and there is a clear feeling of modulation to

[20] *Opere Complete*, xxv, p. 209; unpublished till recent times.

a 'distant' A major and back between bars 34 and 42. Such a feeling of tonal argument is present at the second 'miserere', where a three-part phrase is repeated a fifth lower by a different voice grouping, with an extra counter-theme (Ex. 23). These same devices abound in the Credo,

Ex. 23

too; an extra-modal D major chord is used to paint the word 'passus' (bar 77), along with the more predictable falling and rising scales for 'descendit' and 'ascendit'; and the B flat chord comes twice (bars 127 and 130) on a strong syllable, showing that Palestriná intended a striking effect. His preoccupation with the clarity of high voices can be seen in the fact that all the four-part versets are for SSAT or SSAA (although there is an alternative Christe for ATTB), and that the upper reaches of each voice-range are exploited more than the lower. The Sanctus is perhaps the most varied movement: its flowing phrases are still laid out for different blocks of voices, leading to five simple bars of 'Hosanna', then a florid Benedictus *à 4*, and finally a new Hosanna in triple time. Variety and clarity are the hallmarks of the whole Mass, which is clearly among Palestrina's greatest.

It is a coincidence that all the Masses discussed in detail above are in major modes, Mixolydian or Ionian. The distinctions between these modes became blurred during Palestrina's lifetime by his own accidentals and by obligatory musica ficta so that there is a very real difference between the *Missa L'homme armé* and this *Missa Assumpta est Maria*, where C major is the 'centre' and G major merely the cadence chord, with a feeling of modern major tonality never absent for long. The same is not so true of minor mode works. Here a modality of a more severe kind tends to prevail, in the manner of Palestrina's Franco–Flemish predecessors. There is more distinction between Phrygian, Aeolian, and Dorian modes, and the one closest to the modern minor scale, the Aeolian, is not so frequently found. Sometimes this strong modal feeling is connected with the presence of naturally modal plainsong material: in the two *Missae in Festis Apostolorum*,[21] where plainsong and polyphony alternate, it is especially noticeable, the pure Dorian D minor remaining largely unsullied by B flats and C sharps except at cadences. We might compare these works with a five-part Mass in the Dorian mode by Gombert, the *Missa Media vita*[22] (published 1542). The modality is no more severe than in Palestrina; in fact there is often a richness and warmth of chording compared with which Palestrina's Dorian modality seems a little dry. Ex. 24 shows two passages from

Gombert's Sanctus, the second of which, with its diminished fifth and doubled E natural, sums up the modal qualities of the Mass as a whole. Palestrina's music is drier because the textures are sparser, the voices more spaced out, and the richer dissonances (especially the bass suspension in Ex. 24a, which is a Gombert mannerism) rigorously avoided. On the other hand it is not always as refined as we are sometimes taught, and the quotations that end this chapter (Ex. 25) may serve as a salutary

reminder to teachers of counterpoint that Palestrina was happy to write a dotted minim off the beat, two augmented triads, and, in the third example, an incredible second tenor line. We can ill afford to forget Palestrina's links with the previous Franco–Flemish generation of Gombert, and since it is clearly senseless to criticize Gombert for not having the refinement of a Palestrina, we can learn more by investigating the points of contact between them.

[21] *Opere Complete*, xix, p. 1 and p. 43 respectively.
[22] *Opera Omnia* (Corpus Mensurabilis Musicae 6), ii, p. 1.

III

THE MOTETS

AMONG Palestrina's 250-odd motets, those written for five voices form
the largest body; those for four voices and for double and triple choir
are less numerous, and those in six parts form the smallest group—a
proportion that might surprise us in view of the emphasis on four-part
writing in most manuals of counterpoint.

Palestrina's achievements in the development of the imitative principle which so directly underlies the structure of his motets can be seen
from a study of motets by some of the immediately preceding Franco–
Flemish generation—Goudimel, Clemens non Papa, and Gombert, for
example. The first two of these show a by no means consistent attitude
to the function of imitation. In *Domine ne memineris*[1] by Clemens it is
restricted in scope after the opening point; new themes are not heard
alone, they have accompaniments, and although the last point ('quia
pauperes', bar 42) is repeated at bar 49 to end pars I as a structural
device, SB have a different version of it from AT, and it is not in any
case the first setting of those words (see bar 37) (Ex. 26). Clemens's

Ex. 26   (bar 42)

qui — a paupe – res fa – cti

qui – a pau – pe – res ____ fa – cti sumus

writing sounds continuously spun and non-imitative: new points do not
stand out, for they are not thrown into relief by cadences and a clear
succession of voices entering after rests. Goudimel, representing the
Paris school, is also lax in his treatment of imitation. The opening point
of his *Ista est speciosa*[2] consists of two successive ideas, which occur in
the wrong order in the tenor part; the second point is barely imitated at
all but for its rhythm, and the third generates the rest of pars I, in shapes
varying between ⋀ and ⋏.

[1] *Das Chorwerk*, lxxii.   [2] ibid., ciii.

Gombert's use of imitation is clearer to the ear. Even though his textures are uniformly contrapuntal, individual lines stand out more. In the fine six-part motet *Quem dicunt homines*,[3] for example, it is quite possible to perceive that the fifth and sixth entries occur simultaneously, in parallel fourths, acting as the climax of a beautifully controlled opening. Gombert stands as the direct link between Josquin and Palestrina in the growth of all-pervading imitation. In his hands it became not merely a means of unifying a number of independent strands, but a structural principle. Not only did a number of successive points create a motet, but each individual point might also be treated in various ways within a section. Such was the perfection of the principle that Palestrina inherited, and which informs many of his own motets. Instead of being submerged in a continuously thick texture, his points stand out clearly as they occur; to vary the mode of argument, he may present a double counterpoint—two points simultaneously—of which *Nos autem gloriari*[4] provides the very simple example quoted in Ex. 27. This motet is in fact

Ex. 27

per quem sal-va - - ti

the prototype of the AABBCCDD form, where each point may be slightly varied upon its recurrence. Sometimes a point may be used a third time: this happens to all the points in *Haec dies*,[5] the variations being disposed in the complex form AA'A''BB'CC'B''C''. Palestrina was clearly capable of evolving a long motet from a short text. A long text, with an artificial division into two partes, was by no means as frequent to provide length as it had been in earlier motets.

Other methods of musical structure in Palestrina's motets were connected more directly with the text, which might of itself suggest some kind of refrain form. Several lines of the text of *Tribus miraculis*,[6] for example, begin with the word 'hodie'; thus, each occurrence is set to a falling fifth, unifying each imitation point. A more obvious form, often encountered in the motets of Clemens and Goudimel, is the responsory form ABCB, where two partes end with the same music and text, this 'B' section being of varying length. We have already seen examples of this in works as diverse as Richafort's *Quem dicunt homines*, where only the short Alleluia is repeated, and Palestrina's *Dum complerentur*, where the repeated section contains a complete line of text and a long Alleluia.

[3] *Das Chorwerk*, xciv. [4] *Opere Complete*, iii, p. 82. [5] ibid., xi, p. 66. [6] ibid., iii, p. 15.

Mention might be made, too, of a formal device not dependent upon the text, the repeated final section (ABCC), excellently exemplified in the eight-part *Surge illuminare*,[7] which thus resembles Giovanni Gabrieli in structure as well as in style.

In sacred as in secular music, a distinction has to be made between word painting and mood painting. Neither was the prerogative of secular music in Palestrina's time; it was merely that both were handled with more restraint in sacred music. Word painting is the more artificial compositional procedure, implying the painting of individual words in a phrase or the 'eye music' of the madrigalists, but it could be the vehicle for dramatic expression, as at the climax of Clemens's *Tulerunt autem fratres*[8] (Ex. 28). The text here speaks of Jacob tearing his clothes with

Ex. 28

weeping. Such boldnesses were foreign to the ultra-refined style of Palestrina's motets. For instance, it is tempting though probably unwise to ascribe any pictorial intent to the augmented fourth suspension in the passage from *O Rex gloriae*[9] quoted in Ex. 29, where the text means

Ex. 29

'do not leave us orphans', for it is in the wavy semitones of the soprano line that pathos resides. An excellent example of the different approach to line of Palestrina and Lassus can be seen in two more obvious occasions of word painting shown in Ex. 30.

[7] *Opere Complete*, viii, p. 174.   [8] *Das Chorwerk*, lxxii.   [9] *Opere Complete*, iii, p. 30.

Ex. 30

A (Palestrina: Surge illuminare)

B (Lassus: Surgens Jesus)

Mood painting is an altogether less tangible phenomenon, related sometimes to harmony or modality, but most of all to types of melodic movement. It is now generally accepted that the expression of mood was just as common a feature of sacred music—especially motets—as of secular, from Josquin's time onwards. Once again, we need only look to some motets by the pre-Palestrina generation to be aware of this. Goudimel's *Hodie nobis caelorum rex*[10] expresses a mood of Christmas joy through the sturdy rising phrases or repeated notes of many of its lines, whereas Clemens' *Vox in Rama*[11] is sad not only because of the minor key (which of itself may not tell us anything about mood) but on account of the many falling semitones in melodic ideas, often involving an extra-modal B flat, or the falling phrases of 'Rachel plorans' (bar 42). It is precisely such devices that Palestrina uses to create an extra-ordinarily intense mood of grief in his *Super flumina*.[12] This is quite unparalleled in his other motets, for he usually suppressed the expressive rising minor sixths and the false relations, especially when writing for four parts, and refined various mood-painting devices out of existence. Only in this work is his ascetic craftsmanship matched by a committed fervour. Among four-part motets those of Lassus are more in tune with the times. They have a consistent contrapuntal virtuosity without always depending on the imitative principle; there is also more emphasis on exciting rhythms and sonorities, and the mood of the text is always faithfully expressed, whether it be dramatic and portentous as in *Scio enim*,[13] or joyful as in *Jubilate Deo*.[14] This fervour was inspired by the Counter-Reformation spirit: to find it in Palestrina we need to look to the five-part motets upon texts from the *Song of Songs*. A piece like *Introduxit me rex*[15] shows the weakening of modality by many written-

[10] *Das Chorwerk*, ciii.
[11] ibid., lxxii, and also Davison & Apel, *Historical Anthology of Music*, i, p. 134.
[12] *Opere Complete*, xi, p. 14.
[13] *Sämtliche Werke* (First series), iii, p. 105.
[14] ibid., iii, p. 62.
[15] *Opere Complete*, xi, p. 132.

in accidentals, the use of register contrasts (at the opening) and of angular inner parts, and an abandonment of strict imitation. Even so, Palestrina never came as near to the modern harmonic minor mode as Victoria, whose Tenebrae Responsories[16] contain some of the most expressive music of the time. The expressive devices are just the same as those enumerated above in respect of Clemens, but they are used with a particularly Spanish intensity which is prefigured in the motets of Morales, but is entirely absent from Palestrina's.

With regard to vertical harmony, it is often asserted that Palestrina preferred a greater predominance of full triads than his predecessors. If this is true of his five-part motets, it is not so of the four-part ones, for Gombert, Clemens, Goudimel, and Morales all managed a similar proportion (40–50 per cent on strong beats), and one of Palestrina's forbears of great repute—Willaert—was far more triad-conscious: his *Dilexi quoniam*[17] has an incidence of 80 per cent! He seemed to prefer the 6–5 to the 4–3 suspension, and the effortless euphony of his music was contrived by the constant overlapping of wide leaps in individual parts. To achieve such a thing Palestrina had to resort to a more homophonic approach, as in the presumably late four-part setting of *Alma Redemptoris Mater*.[18] The textures here are bright, and beautifully controlled, and less austere than those of Willaert. In general, Palestrina eschewed the rich and bold dissonances that gave character to the motets of those before him, so that the English cadence formulas, the simultaneous resolutions and false relations, and the double suspensions, were not to be found. One might almost say that it is easier to describe Palestrina's motets by what they did not do rather than by what they did.

What of the difference between the motets of Palestrina and Byrd? Here a more detailed investigation of their respective approaches to two texts—one penitential and one joyous—may prove helpful. Both their settings of *Peccantem me quotidie*[19] are in five parts and in a minor mode. Palestrina prefers the possibilities of sonority to the strict imitative principle: the voices enter quickly, and although the first interval of the 'peccantem' idea varies between a minor third and a minor sixth, the melodies are of restricted span throughout the first twenty-nine bars, having many repeated notes. There are bold harmonic effects in the next section: a sudden flatwards lean at 'timor mortis' whose first minor chord contradicts the previous major one, and is followed by grinding

---

[16] *Opera Omnia*, v.   [17] ibid. (Corpus Mensurabilis Musicae 3), v, p. 8.
[18] ed. H. B. Collins for the series 'Latin Church Music of the Polyphonic Schools'.
[19] *Opere Complete*, vii, p. 98; *Collected Works*, i, p. 138 and *Tudor Church Music*, ix, p. 72.

suspensions (Ex. 31), or the tertial movement of the harmony at 'quia in inferno', which recalls a famous passage with a similar text in Josquin's *Absalon fili mi*[20] (Ex. 32). The last section presents two ideas of

Ex. 31

Ex. 32

contrasted speed which are varied upon repeat, the second one by augmentation, producing a noble conclusion (Ex. 33).

Ex. 33

Byrd's setting is more continuously woven and of greater length, dwelling more upon imitation (though the second point 'et non me paenitentem' is only represented in the tenor by its rising fifth). 'Timor mortis' is given a more restrained setting, though the dissonances brought about by the syncopated 'et salva me' idea add much pathos to the closing passage, culminating in a superb ending (Ex. 34). This example also illustrates the greater feeling for tonality than in Palestrina:

[20] *Werken van Josquin des Pres*, ed. A. Smijers, supplement (Amsterdam, 1969), p.22.

Ex. 34

the motet ends not only with a *tierce de Picardie* but with a whole stretch
of G major (despite E flats), and there are other passages in the middle
where the mode is not merely tinted with A flats, but abandoned in
favour of such keys as B flat, E flat and F minor.

This tendency is confirmed by a comparison between Palestrina's
five-part *Exsultate Deo* and Byrd's *Sing joyfully* (the same text trans-
lated).[21] The former is rooted for the most part in the tonic, whereas the
latter moves more definitely to dominant or subdominant, supertonic or
relative minor, with the return of the 'home key' at 'for this is a statute',
sounding all the stronger for the clear establishment of the dominant
before it (Ex. 35). Both composers show their sure command of sonority,

Ex. 35

[21] *Opere Complete*, xii, p. 88; *Collected Works*, xi, p. 90 and *Tudor Church Music*, ii, p. 288.

made up in Palestrina's case of frequently melismatic strands, in Byrd's of more syllabic ones, as we might expect in a setting of English words. Whereas Palestrina's 'tuba' is a pile-up of rising scales, Byrd's 'trumpet' is more graphically painted by triad motives and a repeated chord (Ex. 36). A study of leaps shows that Byrd is not consistently more angular

Ex. 36

A (Palestrina)

B (Byrd)

than Palestrina, the proportion being much greater in the treble, somewhat greater in the tenor, but not significantly different in the bass.

IV

OTHER LITURGICAL WORKS

PALESTRINA's other sacred works include settings of texts intended for particular liturgical rites, comprising Offertories, Litanies, Hymns, Magnificats, and Lamentations, examples of the last three of which merit some discussion. The Hymns, published in 1589, are the compositions in Palestrina's output most dependent upon a (strophic) plainsong, and represent some interesting examples of a kind of variation technique. Verses are of course sung to alternating polyphony and plainsong, so that the derivation of the one from the other is not only a compositional principle but also becomes perceptible to the listener. Palestrina's normal practice is to set the odd-numbered verses, except the first line of verse 1, which constitutes the plainsong intonation. The basic four-part texture may be diminished to three for one verse, and is usually increased in the final polyphonic verse by way of climax. Palestrina adopts a very flexible attitude to the plainsong: if its phrases are long he prefers to fragment them into more manageable imitative material that can be used in all voices. The old-fashioned cantus firmus treatment is not found, but if any one voice paraphrases the plainsong faithfully it is the treble, where it is most audible. Even so, other voices may derive their lines almost as closely from it. A good example is the severely modal Hymn for the feast of the Transfiguration, *Quicumque Christum quaeritis*,[1] which remains in four parts throughout. Here the imitation points in the treble follow the plainsong closely, if with a little decoration, and the movement varies between cantus firmus-like minims and faster motion. The bass is almost as faithful to the plainsong as the treble. A comparison with the Hymns of Victoria also helps to reveal Palestrina's flexibility of approach. The former lays the plainsong out in long notes in one voice, even in three-part verses, sometimes with counter-themes or chordal movement set against it. The approach is more archaic, but the lines are often more soaring than in Palestrina; they resemble Lassus. This is apparent from their two settings of the Lenten Hymn *Ad preces nostras*.[2] Palestrina appears to have simplified the plainsong considerably (the version is in any case not quite the same) and to have altered the

---

[1] *Opere Complete*, xiv, p. 114.
[2] Palestrina's in *Opere Complete*, xiv, p. 37; Victoria's in *Opera Omnia*, v, p. 17.

mode by changing the final note from G to A. A glance at the beginning of verses 3, 5, 7, and 9 (Ex. 37) will show what variety of imitations are possible with the simple five-note phrase :

Ex. 37

The settings of the Magnificat are less dependent upon plainsong, for as a text this resembles a psalm, and the only melodic content of the Gregorian psalm tones consists in the opening and the inflexions which end the two lines. A particularly good instance of the problems of modality which plainsong created for Palestrina can be studied in the

setting[3] based on Tone 5, which is in the proper Lydian mode with its
B natural (Ex. 38). The opening triad is obviously ideal material for

Ex. 38

imitative treatment, and all but the last of the six polyphonic verses
(even-numbered in this case) open with such imitations. Often the
rhythmic intervals of entry are asymmetrical, but verses 2 and 10
present excellent examples of pair-imitation. In verse 2 the idea is
imitated by inversion in SA, repeated exactly by TB four bars later (Ex.
39). After this Palestrina avoids B flats and moves away from the F major

Ex. 39.

region, veering to C and completing the first lines of the psalm-verses
by introducing short subsidiary ideas: in verse 6 there is a double idea
in invertible counterpoint (Ex. 40). From this point the rest of each

Ex. 40

verse is pervaded by the final inflexion of the psalm tone, whose up-and-
down movement works well in various imitations; from C, he is easily
able to move to A minor or D minor regions to accommodate its B
natural, though the final chord on A may have a C sharp in it which is
contradicted by the succeeding return to F. Only in verse 8 is the complete psalm tone given out in long notes without repetition or trans-
position, whereas in the final verse it appears but sporadically and is not

[3] *Opere Complete*, xvi, p. 147.

imitated; instead a succession of ideas pervades some of the parts, the last of them affording a counterpoint to the final inflexion of the psalm tone (Ex. 41). Instead of reduced-texture verses, Palestrina contrives

Ex. 41

varied sonority by writing verse 6 for AATB, verse 10 for SSAT and the final verse 12 for SATTB. This is a remarkably interesting composition, combining original invention with paraphrase, and exhibiting admirably by its clear sectional form the principles of construction so often employed by its composer.

The settings of the Lamentations constitute liturgical works destined for more restricted usage, namely the rites of Holy Week, like Victoria's Tenebrae Responsories. But unlike Victoria, Palestrina treats the doleful texts of Jeremiah without passion or intensity, in an almost totally impersonal manner. If Hymns and Magnificats are ordinary liturgical entities which offer no particular inspiration to mood painting, the Lamentations are quite another matter. The detached approach that characterizes most of Palestrina's settings makes a considerable contrast with that of most other sixteenth-century masters who set these texts. It is an approach that we have already observed in the motets, and it would be true to say that as a rule Palestrina pays no more heed to the possibilities of these texts than he would to a neutral motet text. Tallis's two sets of Lamentations provide well-known examples of mood painting which abound in felicitous details. But to afford a fairer comparison with Palestrina it would be wiser to examine a comparatively little known five-part set from the Franco–Flemish generation before him, namely one of Crecquillon's.[4] The normal form consists of verses (in the prose style of psalms) each prefaced by a Hebrew letter also set to music, the whole being framed by 'Incipit lamentatio . . .' at the beginning and by 'Jerusalem convertere . . .' at the end. Crecquillon provides four sets; the Hebrew letters are in a flowing polyphonic style usually based upon rising or falling scale figures (Ex. 42). The treble part, rising from F to A, is paraphrasing the plainsong version of the Lamentations, which bears some resemblance to a psalm tone. The verses are sometimes more syllabic, though rarely chordal, and each

---

[4] *Musikalische Denkmäler*, vi, p. 80.

Ex. 42

voice has a splendid rhythmic independence, but the high points are the 'Jerusalem convertere' verses, where the lines are more melodious and conjunct in motion (Ex. 43). Notice the way in which the synco-

Ex. 43

pated idea causes exquisite dissonances in the third and fourth bars.[5] In

[5] See *New Oxford History of Music*, iv, p. 224 for another example of a 'Jerusalem convertere' verse from this work.

fact, the whole work is given life by such dissonances, and yet the melodic lines are beautifully smooth—it is their combination that causes them. Thus, while the work is in the major mode, it has an urgency that befits the text, and shows a command of sonority and line fully equal to that of Palestrina's best work.

Comparable treatment, in mode and texture, can be found in Palestrina's sets 19, 28, and 31, the last two having the same rich voice combination.[6] There is a much greater homogeneity to the music, in that the parts are conceived en bloc and not as a combination of independent, self-sufficient lines. The settings of the Hebrew letters often lack the soaring quality of those by Tallis or Crecquillon, being thought out vertically as a number of superimposed invertible parts (Ex. 44). In this fourfold

Ex. 44

statement there is a 'textural crescendo' (ATB, SSAT, SATB, all) involving its own colour contrasts, and the motives in each of the opening voices are reworked in different ways—*a* and *b* in the second statement with a new suspension idea *d*; *abcd* all together in the third, *b* and *d* in the last. On the other hand the setting of 'Beth' is smoother and more imitative, as in Crecquillon (Ex. 45). Here the bass theme and the falling scales, at first stated in succession, are combined. Palestrina's

Ex. 45

[6] *Opere Complete*, xiii, p. 103, 175, and 198 respectively.

verses are very much more chordal than Crecquillon's, and mainly syllabic; there is little reference to the Gregorian chanting tone on A which is a conspicuous feature in Crecquillon, and very little, as has been stated, of mood painting of a more obvious audible kind. The slow motion and syncopations at 'plorans ploravit' (bar 75 of set 19), followed by falling 6/3 chords, constitute emotional understatement, while the curious harmonic events of a passage from the same verse in set 28—an extra-modal E flat, a (possible) augmented triad, and an unexpected resolution on to C major—may or may not have anything to do with word painting (Ex. 46).

Ex. 46   (bar 75)

It is possible to speculate as to whether Palestrina's uncommitted, impersonal approach to texts of such expressive potential resulted from his having to produce many to order—there are forty-one complete sets—so that the task perhaps palled after a time, or whether it arose out of a deliberate personal decision that any intensity of expression was irreverent or unbecoming in church music. Those who uphold Palestrina as the 'ideal church composer' do so presumably because they hold that the only function of liturgical music is to adorn a text with pleasing melodies and harmonies of an abstract or neutral nature. But, if the Council of Trent welcomed the clear declamation of texts, it also urged that the faithful be uplifted. Other composers—Byrd in his motets, or Victoria in his Tenebrae Responsories, for example—normally achieved this by expressing the text in order to catch the spirit of a particular feastday or church season. They were quite prepared to use the expressive devices common in secular music, which they did not view as 'corrupting influences' in the way that some more sanctimonious church dignitaries[7] have since done. Palestrina seemed to stand apart from these composers. Even if the works which form the subject of the present chapter are pure liturgical *Gebrauchsmusik*, they have a sameness, a dryness of content that is especially surprising in the case of the Lamentations. The most one could say of them is that they are stylistically perfect.

[7] e.g. those responsible for drafting the repressive Vatican *Motu proprio* of 1903.

45

V

THE MADRIGALS

In addition to his prodigious sacred output, Palestrina did find time to compose madrigals. The attitudes to madrigal composition which he struck are somewhat enigmatic, for whereas in prefacing his collection of *Song of Songs* motets in 1584 he renounced the art of setting profane texts, yet only two years later he was back in print with Book II of his secular madrigals, some of these being his finest essays in the medium, enriched indeed by daring harmonies, as we shall see later. For that matter a preface to a volume of *Song of Songs* settings was a curious place to cast aspersions upon the art of madrigal writing, since these very texts are the most madrigalian in the Bible, and the music that adorns them was almost like a sacred transformation of the more modern style of contemporary madrigalists like Marenzio. None the less they remain motets, in which genre they shine when compared with Palestrina's earlier motets, as we have seen. His ambivalent attitude could perhaps have been intended to satisfy at once the public fancy for madrigals— judging by the popularity of Marenzio, another Roman—and the discouragement of such things by the sacred authorities, for Palestrina was an astute man. In fact he published just two collections of madrigals upon profane texts, in 1555 and 1586; the other two collections that have to be mentioned here were of *madrigali spirituali*, a genre beloved of the protagonists of the Counter-Reformation with whom Palestrina needed to ingratiate himself in Rome, for this was the only vernacular music that would have appealed to them.

The long period between the madrigals of the 1550s and 1580s presents an opportunity to assess at a glance the development of Palestrina's maturity in a medium less familiar to him. The first ones appeared at the same time as the more mature madrigals of Arcadelt, the Franco–Fleming who was working in Rome at the time of Palestrina's youth; since each composed a setting of Petrarch's canzona *Chiare fresch'e dolci acque* (an extended poem of five stanzas), a comparison may reveal the approach of the younger composer.[1] Arcadelt's setting is varied in texture, the stanzas being scored respectively for SATTB, ATTB, SAT,

[1] Arcadelt's in A. Einstein, *The Italian Madrigal* (Princeton, 1949), iii, p. 125; Palestrina's in *Opere Complete*, ii, p. 107.

SATB, and SATTB, whereas Palestrina's is in four parts throughout.
The type of writing varies more in Arcadelt's piece, too: majestic polyphony *à 5*, delicate interplay *à 3*, more homophony in the fourth stanza
à 4. Palestrina is less imaginative in these ways but he, like Arcadelt,
uses prolonged syncopation in one voice to build up a climax, as in bars
57 onwards in stanza 3 or bars 69 and 83 onwards in stanza 5; compare
the last ten bars of Arcadelt's stanza 2. And both hit upon remarkably
similar syncopated chords in stanza 4 at the words 'ch'oro forbito e
perle' (Ex. 47). Clearly they must have both been conscious that one

could get away with more when writing madrigals, for Arcadelt uses
chromatic alteration in the top part, and allows momentary consecutive
fifths (often found in the lighter villanelle), while Palestrina makes tell-
ing use of a rising minor sixth in an actual imitation point (Ex. 48), and

of diminished fourths—admittedly editorial but distinctly likely—at the
very end. His last stanza is the best, for not only do we have this, plus
the twice-repeated climax mentioned above, we also perceive a decrease
of motion from the quicker, chattering style that is perhaps too characteristic of the whole piece. It has a sameness and lack of variety noted

47

in the previous chapter; its cadence suspension figures seem a little too mechanical and predictable beside Arcadelt's rolling polyphony.

All this has changed completely in Book II of 1586. In a piece like *Mori quasi il mio core*,[2] the lightweight idiom has all the variety it lacked before. Little two-part ideas have a third voice added to them (bars 6–10), there are expressive falling 6/3 chords (bars 11–15) and although the passage quoted in Ex. 49 may sound four-square, the individual

Ex. 49

lines certainly are not. Reese[3] quotes part of the latter half of this madrigal, which strongly resembles the manner of Byrd with its cross-accents. Not only is there variety within the whole, but also variety within the texture at any given moment, as in Ex. 50, from *I vaghi fiori*,[4]

Ex. 50

with its deliberate, if conventional, contrast between 'grave' semibreves and 'flying' quavers.

The famous *Alla riva del Tebro*[5] represents an altogether more intense style, very rarely encountered in Palestrina, though its very restraint recalls the simplicity of Josquin's wonderful *Absalon fili mi*: it lacks ornament, and has an old-fashioned cadence figure at bars 17–18 (with a surprising resolution). The tensions are largely those of line rather than harmony, as indeed in Josquin: tertial bass lines, rising sixths, falling scales, and so on. Palestrina exploits to the full the technique of combining falling figures with a static pedal note, which he

2 *Opere Complete*, xxxi, p. 44.
3 op. cit., p. 402.
4 *Opere Complete*, xxxi, p. 41.
5 ibid., xxxi, p. 47 and also H.A.M., i, p. 155.

barely uses in his sacred music (Ex. 51). The result is, of course, quite unimaginable in church music, especially that of Palestrina, but it

Ex. 51

shows him to have been capable of such daring discord, which is fascinating and even tantalizing. One might wish that some of the church music had the intensity of this superb madrigal; paradoxically enough it was Victoria, who wrote no madrigals, who brought an emotional expressiveness to church music in Counter-Reformation Rome which Palestrina could not match. Perhaps it was really a case of the character of the man himself—a lover of rigorous discipline and craftsmanlike order who recoiled from overstatement.

VI

CONCLUSION

THE cross-section of Palestrina's works discussed here is a very small part of his output, but it is enough to give us a reasonably balanced view of his position and of his individuality among his forbears and contemporaries. We might equally well have discussed the *Stabat Mater*, some of the Offertories, or the motet *Sicut cervus*; and many more of the Masses could have been mentioned, perhaps even the *Missa Papae Marcelli*, though it is doubtful whether this excellent work occupies the key position in Palestrina's output that some historians have accorded it; the legend that it saved the face of polyphony in the eyes of the Council of Trent has long been rejected.

To what extent was Palestrina a conservative composer? Reese, in his masterly appraisal of Palestrina's historical position, shows how many have asserted his conservatism because they approached his music via the manuals of counterpoint and found that, in general, he conforms to their precepts.[1] But if Palestrina were conservative, we should expect his music not to differ from that of Gombert or Morales, whereas Reese rightly points out that he represents the *last* stage in the formulation of dissonance treatment. In this context it is hard to understand Curt Sachs' remark, quoted by Reese, that Palestrina 'resumed the Josquin style of 1500 with its predilection for symmetrical structure and quiet harmonies and gave it an austere serenity . . .' Josquin's harmonies were not by any means quiet: Palestrina's achievement was to smooth them over. Even so, Josquin's name has been invoked from time to time in these pages in order to show Palestrina's connection with the central polyphonic style of the high Renaissance.

Lang, another eminent historian writing in fairly recent times about Palestrina, sees his art as much more modern in spirit, but holds that his historical position was peripheral beside the culmination of Franco–Flemish polyphony in Lassus and Monte.[2] The implications of the latter point are worth investigating. It is after all more logical historically, being also a welcome antidote to the notion that all polyphonic paths lead to Palestrina as all roads lead to Rome. It prompts one to see

[1] Reese, *Music in the Renaissance*, p. 459 ff.
[2] *Music in Western Civilization* (London, 1942), p. 232 ff.

Palestrina as a man who stood somewhat apart from the mainstream in his ultra-refined treatment of dissonance and his almost total reluctance to use it for emotional ends. Yet this conflicts with Lang's further observations that his works were not anaemic and expressionless but glowed with faith and passion, foreshadowing the Baroque. If Palestrina did look forward, it was in his changing attitude to textures and his growing predilection for homophony, not in passion or emotionalism.

A more objective view is proposed by Grout, who considers his music to represent the conservative side of the Counter-Reformation.[3] Its other, more aggressive and outgoing side inspired the music of Lassus, Victoria, and the Venetians; it fostered the growth of the *stile moderno* of the early Baroque, which carried sacred music forward just as it did secular, relegating the *stile antico* to second place, where it became ossified and self-consciously archaic in expression. The Counter-Reformation was bound to have a more introspective, conservative aspect, especially in Rome, centre of the Church's government. Grout also mentions Palestrina's debt to plainchant, which was considerable: when we remember that the models of many parody Masses were motets based in their turn upon plainchant, and add to them all the paraphrase and other Masses based upon it, we can see that he owed more to it than any other sixteenth-century polyphonist. It must be admitted that the chant was in a decadent state at the time—hence the normally high proportion of parody Masses *not* related to plainsong in the output of other composers—and that Palestrina was one of those charged to reform it. In his capacity as master of music at the Roman Seminary, he taught plainsong. His avowed contact with this timeless art of the church has undoubtedly been one of the reasons for the fanatical adulation of his music by the Vatican powers-that-be, especially in the last hundred years, which have seen the resuscitation of plainsong. This has contributed as much as any other factor to the lack of an objective view of Palestrina's music.

The true precursors of the spirit of the Baroque were those who invested their church music with an emotional fervour and who heralded the breakdown of the conventional laws of dissonance treatment in the quest for a more graphic presentation of the text. The style of Palestrina survived him in the hands of his more conservative Roman imitators and those elsewhere who could not keep pace with modernism, to become accepted as the *stile antico*. It co-existed happily alongside the modern style, being ordinarily reserved for simpler Mass and psalm music for everyday use, where the texts did not invite a bold modern

[3] *A History of Western Music* (London, 1962), p. 238 ff.

setting. It could easily be distinguished from the more up-to-date manner by its alla breve notation and close adherence to Palestrinian dissonance treatment. In this form the style became the basis for Fux's manual of counterpoint in the mid-eighteenth century, even though the true spirit of Renaissance polyphony was a thing of the distant past. The rediscovery of Palestrina's actual music by sentimental nineteenth-century historians, at a time when musicology was in its infancy, made an objective assessment of his output difficult to achieve until recent times.

The truth is that Palestrina was not a conservative because he conformed to the 'rules': in any case, the only rules worthy of consideration are those of contemporary theorists like Zarlino, who talked about avoiding fifths and octaves, extolled the virtues of good chord-spacing, enumerated all the artful contrapuntal procedures, but went no further. Neither was Palestrina a conservative because his style stood still between early and late works: within certain limits, it changed gradually in his lifetime as in that of any composer who lives to three-score-and-ten years, so that in some respects his later works do look forward to the Baroque. His dissonance treatment is, if not an advance, certainly a refinement—indeed an ultra-refinement—of that of his predecessors. And he was not a conservative merely because he wrote mainly church music: Victoria or Schütz were later composers who achieved fame in the same way. Palestrina was behind the times because he was so closely tied to Rome; unlike Victoria or Lassus, who came there for short periods, he was beholden to the Church authorities to a much greater extent, even if the Popes were not his only employers. He was a conservative in his deliberate preference for writing Masses, whose abstract text he could clothe in equally abstract polyphony, and for drawing upon plainsong or his own motets (or both) for the musical fabric of these Masses, rather than motets or secular music by others. Apart from a few notable exceptions, his other church music shows little response to the text compared with the work of his contemporaries. Even if his growing use of chordal and note-against-note writing rendered the text clearer to the ear, in accordance with the wishes of the Council of Trent, the possibility of adorning it with musical mood painting (where appropriate) remained distasteful to him; the abstract polyphony of the Masses, wonderfully craftsmanlike as it is, served Palestrina equally well for most other sacred texts. With regard to his madrigals, one can agree with Denis Arnold that he was not only behind the times, but living in another world.[4] The result is a corpus of music, much of it beautiful to

4 *Marenzio* (London, 1965), p. 5.

the ear, in which one piece sounds very much like another. This could never be said of Victoria, Lassus, or Byrd. The versatility of the latter two was alien to Palestrina; he distrusted the adventurous spirit of his day, preferring the cosy confines of Rome and his abstract polyphonic style (and asking impossible salaries of any prospective patron who tried to lure him away from there). His Masses will always show the height of his greatness, for they grew most naturally out of his environment. Perhaps we cannot honestly acclaim him as the supreme master, who stood above Lassus, Byrd, or even Victoria, nor assert that Josquin or Gombert were inferior just because their technique was less refined.

But, being more familiar with the work of his contemporaries and predecessors, we can now view him as one among equals, and appreciate with greater discrimination the particular character of his music, the stature of individual works in his output, and the greatness of his achievement as a whole.

LIST OF PUBLICATIONS

1554   *Missarum Liber Primus*, Rome, Dorico.
One madrigal in *De diversi autori il quarto libro de madrigali a quatro voci*, Venice, Gardano.

1555   *Il Primo Libro di Madrigali a 4 voci*, Rome, Dorico.

1557   One madrigal in *Di Cipriano de Rore il secondo libro de madregali a quatro voci*, Venice, Gardano.

1558   Three madrigals in *Secondo libro delle muse*, Rome, Barré.

1559   One madrigal in *Il secondo libro delle Muse*, Venice, Gardano.

1560   One madrigal in *Madrigali a cinque voci d'Alessandro Striggio*, Venice, Scotto.

1561   Eight madrigals in *Il terzo libro delle Muse*, Venice, Gardano.

1562   Three madrigals in *Il terzo libro delle Muse*, Rome, Barré.
One madrigal in *Di Francesco Roselli il primo libro de madrigali*, Venice, Gardano.

1563   *Motecta Festorum totius anni quaternis vocibus . . . Liber Primus*, Rome, Dorico.
Two motets in *Liber primus Musarum*, Venice, Rampazetto.

1564   Reprint of *Motecta Liber Primus*, Venice, Gardano.

1566   One madrigal in *Il Desiderio*, Venice, Scotto.
One madrigal in *Di Cipriano de Rore il quinto libro di madrigali a cinque voci*, Venice, Gardano.

1567   *Missarum Liber Secundus*, Rome, Dorico.

1568   Reprint of *Il Primo Libro di Madrigali*, Venice, Merulo.
Reprint of *Missarum Liber Secundus*, Venice, Gardano.
One madrigal in *Corona della morte*, Venice, Scotto.

1569   *Liber Primus Motettorum quae partim quinis, partim senis, partim septenis v. concinantur*, Rome, Dorico.

1570   *Missarum Liber Tertius*, Rome, Dorico.
Reprint of *Il Primo Libro di Madrigali*, Venice, Vincenti.
Reprint of *Missarum Liber Secundus*, Rome, Dorico.
One madrigal in *I dolci frutti*, Venice, Scotto.
Seven madrigals in *Prima Stella*, Venice, Scotto.

1571   Reprint of *Motecta Liber Primus*, Venice, Gardano.

1572   *Motettorum quae partim quinis, partim senis, partim Octonis v. concinantur Lib. secundus*, Venice, Scotto.
Reprint of *Missarum Liber Primus*, Rome, Dorico.

1573   Reprint of *Motettorum Lib. secundus*, Venice, Scotto.

1574   Reprint of *Il Primo Libro di Madrigali*, Venice, Merulo.
Reprint of *Motecta Liber Primus*, Venice, Gardano.
Four madrigals in *Il quarto libro delle muse*, Venice, Gardano.

1575   *Motettorum quae partim quinis, partim senis, partim octonis v concinantur Lib. tertius*, Venice, Scotto.
Reprint of *Motecta Liber Primus*, Venice, Scotto.
Reprints of *Missarum Liber Tertius*, Rome, Gardano, and Venice, Scotto.
Reprint of *Motettorum Lib. tertius*, Rome, Gardano.

1576   Two madrigals in *Musica di XIII. autori*, Venice, Gardano.

1577   Reprint of *Motettorum Lib. secundus*, Venice, Scotto.
One madrigal in *Il primo fiore della ghirlanda musicale*, Venice, Scotto.

1579   Reprint of *Motecta Liber Primus*, Venice, Gardano.
Reprint of *Liber Primus Motettorum*, Venice, Gardano.

1580   Reprint of *Motettorum Lib. secundus*, Venice, Scotto.

1581   *Il primo Lib. de Madrigali a cinque v.*, Venice, Gardano.
Motettorum quatuor v. partim plena v. et partim paribus v. Liber Secundus, Venice, Gardano.
Reprint of *Motettorum Lib. tertius*, Venice, Scotto.

1582   *Missarum cum quatuor et quinque v. Lib. Quartus*, Venice, Gardano.
Reprint of *Missarum Liber Tertius*, Rome, Gardano.
Reprint of *Missarum Lib. Quartus*, Rome, Gardano.

1583   Reprint of *Il Primo Libro di Madrigali*, Venice, Vincenti.
Reprint of *Motettorum Lib. secundus*, Venice, Scotto.
Three motets in *Il primo libro delle laude*, Rome, Gardano.
One madrigal in *Li amorosi ardori*, Venice, Gardano.
One madrigal in *Harmonia celeste*, Antwerp, Phalèse.
One madrigal in *Musica divina*, Antwerp, Phalèse.

1584   *Motettorum quinque v. Lib quartus ex Canticis Canticorum*, Venice, Gardano.
Motettorum quinque v. Lib. quintus, Rome, Gardano.
Reprint of *Motettorum Lib. quartus*, Rome, Gardano.
Reprint of *Motettorum Lib. quintus*, Venice, Gardano.
One madrigal in *Spoglia amorosa*, Venice, Scotto.
Five madrigals in *Fronimo dialogo*, Venice, Scotto.

1585   Reprints of *Motecta Liber Primus*, Venice, Gardano, and Rome, Gardano.
Eight motets in *Sacrae cantiones*, Nürnberg, Gerlach.

One Mass in *Di . . . Palestrina una messa*, Venice, Scotto.
One madrigal in *De floridi virtuosi . . . il secondo libro de madrigali*, Venice, Amadino.

1586 *Il secundo Lib. de Madrigali a quatro v.*, Venice, Scotto.
Reprint of *Missarum Liber Primus*, Venice, Gardano.
Reprint of *Liber Primus Motettorum*, Venice, Scotto.
Three canzonets in *Diletto spirituale*, Rome, van Buyten.
One madrigal in *De floridi virtuosi . . . il terzo libro de madrigali*, Venice, Amadino.
One madrigal in *Corona de dodici sonetti*, Venice, Gardano.

1587 Reprint of *Il Primo Libro di Madrigali*, Venice, Amadino.
Reprint of *Motectorum Liber Secundus*, Milan, Tini.
Reprints of *Motettorum Lib. Quartus*, Venice, Gardano, and Milan, Tini.
Five madrigals in *Il quarto libro delle Muse*, Milan, Tini.

1588 *Lamentationum Hieremiae Prophetae Lib. Primus*, Rome, Gardano.
Reprint of *Il primo Libro di Madrigali*, Venice, Vincenti.
Reprint of *Motettorum Lib. secundus*, Venice, Scotto.
Reprint of *Motectorum Liber Secundus*, Venice, Scotto.
Reprint of *Motettorum Lib. quartus*, Venice, Vincenti.
Reprint of *Motettorum Lib. quintus*, Venice, Scotto.
One madrigal in *Giardinetto de madrigali*, Venice, Amadino.
Three madrigals in *Gemma musicalis*, Nürnberg, Gerlach.
Five madrigals in *Musica transalpina*, London, East.

1589 *Hymni totius anni . . . quatuor v. concinendi*, Rome, Coattino, and Venice, Gardano.
Reprint of *Motettorum Lib. tertius*, Venice, Scotto.
Reprint of *Lamentationum Lib. Primus*, Venice, Scotto.
One madrigal in *Le gioie*, Venice, Amadino.
Two madrigals in *Ghirlanda di fioretti*, Rome, Verovio.
Two madrigals in *Musicale essercitio*, Venice, Gardano.

1590 *Missarum quatuor, quinque ac sex v. concinendarum Lib. quintus*, Rome, Coattino.
Reprint of *Missarum Liber Primus*, Venice, Vincenti.
Reprint of *Motecta Liber Primus*, Rome, Coattino.
Reprint of *Liber Primus Motettorum*, Venice, Gardano.
Reprint of *Motectorum Liber Secundus*, Rome, Coattino.
Reprint of *Missarum Lib. Quartus*, Milan, Tini.
Reprint of *Hymni totius anni*, Venice, Scotto.
One Mass in *Missae quinque*, Nürnberg, Gerlach.

Ten motets in *Corollarium cantionum sacrarum*, Nürnberg, Gerlach.

Some motets in *Suavissimorum modulorum*, Munich, Berg.

1591 *Magnificat octo tonum Lib. Primus*, Rome, Gardano, and Venice, Gardano.

Reprints of *Missarum Liber Primus*, Rome, Gardano, and Venice, Scotto.

Reprint of *Motettorum Lib. quintus*, Venice, Scotto.

Reprint of *Missarum Lib. quintus*, Venice, Scotto.

Three madrigals in *Melodia olympica*, Antwerp, Phalèse.

Two canzonets in *Canzonette a quattro voci*, Rome, Verovio.

Two canzonets in *Canzonette . . . Libro primo*, Venice, Vincenti.

1592 One Mass in *Missae dominicales*, Milan, Tini.

One piece in *Psalmi Motecta, Magnificat*, Rome, Coattino.

One madrigal in *Il trionfo di Dori*, Venice, Gardano.

One madrigal in *De' floridi virtuosi. Il secondo libro de' madrigali* (reprint), Venice, Vincenti.

One madrigal in *Spoglia amorosa* (reprint), Venice, Gardano.

1593 *Offertoria totius anni*, Rome, Coattino, and Venice, Gardano.

Reprint of *Il primo Lib. de Madrigali*, Venice, Gardano.

Reprint of *Motettorum Lib. quartus*, Milan, Tini.

Reprint of *Il secundo Lib. de Madrigali*, Venice, Gardano.

One madrigal in *Florindo, e Armilla canzon pastorale*, Venice, Amadino.

Three madrigals in *Nuova spoglia amorosa*, Venice, Vincenti.

1594 *Delle Madrigali Spirituali a cinque v. . . . Lib. Sec.*, Rome, Coattino.

Missae quinque, quatuor ac quinque v. concinendae . . . Lib. Sextus, Rome, Coattino.

Missae quinque, quatuor ac quinque v. concinendae . . . Lib. septimus, Rome, Coattino.

Reprint of *Il Primo Libro di Madrigali*, Venice, Gardano.

Reprint of *Missarum Liber Tertius*, Venice, Gardano.

Reprint of *Mottetorum Lib. secundus*, Venice, Gardano.

Reprint of *Motettorum Lib. tertius*, Venice, Gardano.

Reprint of *Offertoria totius anni*, Venice, Gardano.

1595 Reprint of *Motecta Liber Primus*, Venice, Scotto.

Reprint of *Motettorum Lib. quintus*, Venice, Gardano.

Reprint of *Missae Lib. septimus*, Rome, Coattino.

1596 Reprint of *Missarum Liber Primus*, Venice, Gardano.

Reprint of *Il Primo Libro di Madrigali*, Venice, Scotto.

Reprint of *Missarum Liber Tertius*, Venice, Gardano.
Reprints of *Motectorum Liber Secundus*, Venice, Gardano and Scotto.
Reprint of *Motettorum Lib. quartus*, Venice, Scotto.
Reprint of *Offertoria totius anni*, Venice, Gardano.
Reprint of *Missae Lib. Sextus*, Venice, Gardano.
Ten litanies in *Thesaurus litaniarum*, Munich, Berg.
Six pieces in *Responsoria antiphonae, et hymni*, Rome, Mutio.
One madrigal in *Paradiso musicale*, Antwerp, Phalèse.
Two madrigals in *Vittoria amorosa*, Venice, Vincenti.

1597 Two madrigals in *Il vago alboreto*, Antwerp, Phalèse.

1598 Reprint of *Missarum Liber Secundus*, Venice, Gardano.
Reprint of *Missarum Liber Tertius*, Venice, Gardano.
Four motets in *Sacrae symphoniae*, Nürnberg, Kaufmann.

1599 *Missarum cum quatuor, quinque et sex v. Lib. Octavus*, Venice, Scotto.
Missarum cum quatuor, quinque et sex v. Lib. Nonus, Venice, Scotto.
Missarum cum quatuor, quinque et sex v. Lib. Decimus, Venice, Scotto.
Reprints of *Missarum Liber Secundus*, Venice, Gardano, and Rome, Mutio.
Reprint of *Missarum Liber Tertius*, Venice, Gardano.
One Mass in *Selectissimarum missarum flores*, Antwerp, Phalèse.
One motet in *Motetti et salmi*, Venice, Vincenti.
Two motets in *Motetti di Orfeo Vecchi . . . Libro primo*, Milan, Tini & Besozzi.

1600 *Missarum cum quatuor, quinque et sex v. Lib. Undecimus*, Venice, Scotto.
Reprint of *Missarum Liber Secundus*, Rome, Mutio.
Reprint of *Liber Primus Motettorum*, Venice, Scotto.
Reprint of *Missarum Lib. Nonus*, Venice, Scotto.
Reprint of *Missarum Lib. Decimus*, Venice, Scotto.
One motet in *Sacrarum symphoniarum continuatio*, Nürnberg, Kaufmann.
Four madrigals in *De floridi virtuosi . . . madrigali a cinque voci*, Antwerp, Phalèse.
Two motets in *Della nova Metamorfosi*, Milan, Tradate.

1601 *Missarum cum quatuor, quinque et sex v. Lib. Duodecimus*, Venice, Scotto.
Missae quatuor octonis v. concinendae. Venice, Amadino.

Reprint of *Motecta Liber Primus*, Venice, Gardano.

Reprint of *Motettorum Lib. quartus*, Venice, Gardano.

Reprint of *Motettorum Lib. quintus*, Venice, Scotto.

1603 Reprint of *Motettorum Lib. quartus*, Venice, Scotto.

Reprint of *Offertoria totius anni*, Antwerp, Phalèse.

1604 Reprint of *Motectorum Liber Secundus*, Venice, Gardano.

Reprint of *Il primo Lib. de Madrigali*, Venice, Gardano.

One madrigal in *Scielta de madrigali*, Milan, Tini and Lomazzo.

1605 Reprint of *Il Primo Libro di Madrigali*, Venice, Gardano.

Reprint of *Motettorum Lib. quartus*, Antwerp, Phalèse.

Reprint of *Missae Lib. septimus*, Venice, Gardano.

One motet in *Triodia sacra*, Dillingen, Meltzer.

One motet in *Della nova Metamorfosi . . . Libro secondo*, Milan, Tradate.

One madrigal in *Nervi d'Orfeo*, Leiden, de' Haestens.

1606 Reprint of *Motectorum Liber Secundus*, Venice, Scotto.

Two motets in *Hortus musicalis*, Pavia, Nenninger.

1607 One motet in *Musarum Sioniar*, Nürnberg, Wagenmann.

1608 Reprint of *Missarum Liber Primus*, Rome, Dorico.

Reprints of *Motettorum Lib. quartus*, Venice, Gardano and Raverii.

Reprint of *Missarum Lib. Nonus*, Venice, Scotto.

Two canzonets in *Newe teutsche Canzonetten*, Frankfurt, Richter.

1609 Reprint of *Missae Lib. septimus*, Venice, Scotto.

Reprint of *Missarum Lib. Octavus*, Venice, Scotto.

One motet in *Florilegium sacrarum cantionum*, Antwerp, Phalèse.

1610 Reprint of *Missarum Lib. Quartus*, Milan, Tini and Lomazzo.

1612 One motet in *Promptuarii musici . . . pars altera*, Strasbourg, Kieffer.

1613 Reprint of *Motecta Liber Primus*, Antwerp, Phalèse.

Reprints of *Motettorum Lib. quartus*, Venice, Magni and Gardano.

One motet in *Promptuarii musici . . . pars tertia*, Strasbourg, Kieffer.

One madrigal in *Rest musicalisches Streitkränzleins*, Nürnberg, Scherff.

1614 Three motets in *Selectae cantiones*, Rome, Zannetti.

1616 Some motets in *Les Rossignols spirituels*, Valenciennes, Vervliet.

1617 Two motets in *Promptuarii musici . . . pars quarta*, Strasbourg, Bertram.

1619 Three Masses in *Messe a quattro voci*, Rome, Soldi.

One madrigal in *Triumphi di Dorothea*, Leipzig, Köber.

1620   Reprint of *Missarum Liber Tertius*, Venice, Gardano.

One work in *Scelta de Salmi . . . Libro quinto*, Orvieto, Zannetti.

1621   Three motets in *Sacrae cantiones*, Antwerp, Phalèse.

1625   Reprint of *Hymni totius anni*, Rome, Soldi.

1639   One work in *Salmi, magnificat, e motetti*, Orvieto, Ruuli.

1644   Reprint of *Hymni totius anni*, Antwerp, Moreto.

1650   Reprint of *Motettorum Lib. quartus*, Rome, Mascardi.

SELECT BIBLIOGRAPHY

Apart from items referred to in footnotes, the following are recommended:

Andrews, H. K., *An Introduction to the Technique of Palestrina* (London, 1958).

Einstein, A., *The Italian Madrigal* (Princeton, 1949).

Fellerer, K. G., *Palestrina* (Regensburg, 1930; rev. and enlarged ed., Düsseldorf, 1960).

Hamburger, P., 'The Ornamentations in the Works of Palestrina', *Acta Musicologica*, xxii (1950).

Jeppesen, K., *The Style of Palestrina and the Dissonance* (Copenhagen and London, 1946).

Jeppesen, K., 'The Recently Discovered Mantova Masses of Palestrina', *Acta Musicologica*, xxii (1950).

Jeppesen, K., 'Some Remarks to "The Ornamentations in the Works of Palestrina" by Poul Hamburger', *Acta Musicologica*, xxii (1950).

Roche, J., *The Madrigal* (London, 1972).

Tovey, D. F., 'Wilbye and Palestrina: four sixteenth-century motets', *Essays in Musical Analysis*, vol. 5 (London, 1937), pp. 12ff.